D0319681

THE
Irish Pub
COOKBOOK

This edition published in 2011
LOVE FOOD is an imprint of Parragon Books Ltd

Parragon
Queen Street House
4 Queen Street
Bath BA1 1HE, UK

Copyright © Parragon Books Ltd 2010

LOVE FOOD and the accompanying heart device is a registered trade
mark of Parragon Books Ltd in Australia, the UK, USA, India and the
EU.

All rights reserved. No part of this publication may be reproduced,
stored in a retrieval system or transmitted, in any form or by any means,
electronic, mechanical, photocopying, recording or otherwise, without
the prior permission of the copyright holder.

ISBN: 978-1-4454-4454-3

Printed in China

Notes for the Reader
This book uses both metric and imperial measurements. Follow
the same units of measurement throughout; do not mix metric and
imperial. All spoon measurements are level: teaspoons are assumed to
be 5 ml, and tablespoons are assumed to be 15 ml. Unless otherwise
stated, milk is assumed to be full fat, eggs and individual vegetables
are medium, and pepper is freshly ground black pepper.

The times given are an approximate guide only. Preparation times differ
according to the techniques used by different people and the cooking
times may also vary from those given. Optional ingredients, variations
or serving suggestions have not been included in the calculations.

Recipes using raw or very lightly cooked eggs should be avoided
by infants, the elderly, pregnant women, convalescents and anyone
suffering from an illness. Pregnant and breastfeeding women are
advised to avoid eating peanuts and peanut products. Sufferers from
nut allergies should be aware that some of the ready-made ingredients
used in the recipes in this book may contain nuts. Always check the
packaging before use.

Picture acknowledgements
The publisher would like to thank Getty Images for permission to
reproduce copyright material: Cover (1st row left & right; 2nd row
left & right; 4th row left; 5th row centre) and pages 5 (centre),
7, 10, 22, 27, 33, 45, 46, 51, 57, 63, 65, 71, 77 & 78.

Contents

Introduction

The traditional Irish pub has a long and venerable history. From quaint country taverns with their thatched roofs and cosy snugs to metropolitan bars with their Victorian wood panelling and patterned tiled floors, pubs in Ireland have long been places of sanctuary where people of all classes and creeds can go to forget their everyday cares, engage in lively banter and share a beverage or two in an atmosphere of relaxed conviviality. They also play an important role in community life to the extent that, still today, some rural and market-town pubs double up as the village shop, post office or even undertakers. Such is the appeal of the authentic Irish pub that bars in many international cities have attempted to replicate its essential charm, with varying degrees of success!

Yet there is more to the Irish pub than drinking and revelry. Today, many pubs across the Emerald Isle are popular eating establishments in their own right, serving both familiar favourites and more contemporary dishes. While it may not be possible to recreate the ambience of a traditional Irish pub in your own home, you can certainly experience a taste of Irish pub cuisine by sampling the recipes in this book. Conveniently split into four chapters that follow the course of a typical meal, this book contains all the recipes you will need to cook up an Irish-style feast. In Starters & Snacks, you will find a range of dishes that would be ideal for a light lunch or the first course of a more substantial meal. Main Courses contains recipes for homely stews, casseroles and pies that are guaranteed to warm you up on a cold winter's day. In Vegetables & Sides, there are a whole host of vegetable dishes, as well as breads and other savoury snacks. Finally, Desserts & Drinks contains a selection of hot and cold desserts, plus a couple of drinks — the perfect way to round off any meal.

Chapter 1
STARTERS & SNACKS

Leek & Potato Soup

Leeks and potatoes are staples in Irish cuisine. For cooking, small, tender leeks are better than huge ones. This soup can be roughly blended to give a hearty, country texture or processed until smooth and served with cream and snipped chives for a more luxurious soup.

Serves 4–6

55 g/2 oz butter
1 onion, chopped
3 leeks, sliced
225 g/8 oz potatoes, cut into 2-cm/
  $^{3}/_{4}$-inch cubes
850 ml/1$^{1}/_{2}$ pints vegetable stock
salt and pepper
150 ml/5 fl oz single cream (optional),
  to serve
2 tbsp snipped fresh chives, to garnish

❋ Melt the butter in a large saucepan over a medium heat, add the prepared vegetables and sauté gently for 2–3 minutes, until soft but not brown. Pour in the stock and bring to the boil, then reduce the heat and simmer, covered, for 15 minutes.

❋ Remove from the heat and liquidize the soup in the saucepan using a hand-held stick blender if you have one. Alternatively, pour into a blender, liquidize until smooth and return to the rinsed-out saucepan.

❋ Reheat the soup and season to taste with salt and pepper. Ladle into warmed bowls and serve, swirled with the cream, if using, and garnished with the chives.

Smoked Cod Chowder

With its hundreds of miles of coastline, it is no wonder that Ireland is famous for its fabulous fish and seafood. This recipe uses smoked cod, which gives the chowder a wonderfully rich flavour.

Serves 4

25 g/1 oz butter
1 onion, finely chopped
1 small celery stick, finely diced
250 g/9 oz potatoes, diced
55 g/2 oz carrots, diced
300 ml/10 fl oz boiling water
350 g/12 oz smoked cod fillets, skinned and cut into bite-sized pieces
300 ml/10 fl oz milk
salt and pepper
fresh flat-leaf parsley sprigs, to garnish

- Melt the butter in a large saucepan over a low heat, add the onion and celery and cook, stirring frequently, for 5 minutes, or until soft but not brown.
- Add the potatoes, carrots, water and salt and pepper to taste. Bring to the boil, then reduce the heat and simmer for 10 minutes, or until the vegetables are tender. Add the fish to the chowder and cook for a further 10 minutes.
- Pour in the milk and heat gently. Taste and adjust the seasoning, adding salt and pepper if necessary. Ladle into warmed bowls and serve, garnished with parsley sprigs.

MUSSENDEN TEMPLE, COUNTY DERRY

Split Pea & Ham Soup

This heart-warming soup benefits from the long, slow cooking process used in this recipe. It is a great way to use up any leftover ham and is perfect on its own as a light lunch or served with bread for a filling and satisfying main meal.

Serves 6–8

500 g/1 lb 2 oz split green peas
1 tbsp olive oil
1 large onion, finely chopped
1 large carrot, finely chopped
1 celery stick, finely chopped
1 litre/1³/₄ pints chicken or vegetable stock
1 litre/1³/₄ pints water
225 g/8 oz lean smoked ham, finely diced
¹/₄ tsp dried thyme
¹/₄ tsp dried marjoram
1 bay leaf
salt and pepper

❧ Rinse the peas under cold running water. Put in a saucepan and cover generously with water. Bring to the boil and boil for 3 minutes, skimming off the foam from the surface. Drain the peas.

❧ Heat the oil in a large saucepan over a medium heat. Add the onion and cook for 3–4 minutes, stirring occasionally, until just softened.

❧ Add the carrot and celery and continue cooking for 2 minutes. Add the peas, pour in the stock and water and stir to combine.

❧ Bring just to the boil and stir the ham into the soup. Add the thyme, marjoram and bay leaf. Reduce the heat, cover and cook gently for 1–1¹/₂ hours, until the ingredients are very soft. Remove and discard the bay leaf.

❧ Taste and adjust the seasoning, adding salt and pepper if necessary. Ladle into warmed bowls and serve.

Rye Toast with Roast Beef & Coleslaw

Beef and cabbage is a classic and very tasty combination, as demonstrated by this chunky beef sandwich with home-made coleslaw. You can use any leftover corned beef (see page 28) in place of the roast beef.

Serves 1

1 tbsp finely chopped fresh ginger or
  horseradish sauce
20 g/³/₄ oz butter, softened
2 slices light rye bread
1 very thin slice cabbage (white or firm
  green heart)
1 small carrot, coarsely grated
1 spring onion, sliced
1 large slice roast beef
salt and pepper
gherkins, to serve (optional)

❁ Preheat the grill to medium–high. Mix the ginger with the butter.

❁ Spread one slice of bread generously with some of the butter. Top with the cabbage, trimming any overhanging shreds and placing them back on the middle of the sandwich. Top with carrot and spring onion, keeping them away from the edge. Season lightly with salt and pepper.

❁ Spread a little more of the butter on one side of the beef and lay it, butter side down, on the carrot. Spread the remaining butter on the second slice of bread and place it on top of the sandwich, butter side down.

❁ Toast the sandwich under the preheated grill on both sides, until crisp and golden. Serve immediately with gherkins, if using.

Glazed Beetroot & Egg Sourdough Toasts

With its vibrant colour and sweet flavour, beetroot looks just as good as it tastes. In this recipe, it is partnered by chopped boiled eggs to make a tasty toast topping. When cooking fresh beetroot, leave 2.5 cm/1 inch of stem attached to prevent the colour from 'bleeding' and peel after cooking.

Serves 2–4

4 eggs
500 g/1 lb 2 oz cooked beetroot (fresh or vacuum-packed without vinegar)
2 tsp sugar, or to taste
5 tsp cider vinegar, or to taste
4 slices sourdough bread
6 tbsp olive oil
1 tbsp Dijon mustard
3 tbsp chopped fresh dill
salt and pepper

- Cook the eggs in a pan of boiling water for 8 minutes, then drain, shell and chop them. Set aside. Dice the beetroot quite small and place in a small bowl. Mix in half the sugar and 1 teaspoon of the vinegar and season to taste with salt and pepper.
- Preheat the grill to medium–high. Brush the bread with a little of the oil and toast under the preheated grill for 2–3 minutes, until crisp and golden.
- Meanwhile, drizzle 1 teaspoon of the remaining oil over the beetroot. Whisk together the remaining vinegar and sugar with the mustard and salt and pepper to taste. Gradually whisk in the remaining oil to make a thick dressing. Stir in the dill and taste for seasoning – it should be sweet and mustardy, with a sharpness – add more sugar or vinegar if you wish.
- Turn the bread over and top with the beetroot, giving it a stir first, covering the slices right up to the crusts. Glaze the beetroot under the grill for 2–3 minutes, until browned in places.
- Cut the slices in half or quarters and top with the reserved chopped egg. Drizzle with a little dressing and serve immediately.

Blue Cheese & Walnut Tartlets

So lush and green are the pasture lands that Irish dairy herds graze upon that it is no surprise that the resulting cheeses are of equally fine quality. Try using an Irish blue cheese, such as Cashel Blue, to make these tartlets. Many Irish cheeses are available worldwide in supermarkets and speciality stores.

Makes 12

Pastry
225 g/8 oz plain flour, plus extra
   for dusting
pinch of celery salt
100 g/3^1/$_2$ oz cold butter, cut into pieces,
   plus extra for greasing
25 g/1 oz walnut halves, very finely
   chopped

Filling
25 g/1 oz butter
2 celery sticks, trimmed and finely
   chopped
1 small leek, trimmed and finely
   chopped
200 g/7 oz blue cheese
200 ml/7 fl oz double cream,
   plus 2 tbsp extra
3 egg yolks
salt and pepper

❁ Lightly grease 12 x 7.5-cm/3-inch holes in a muffin tin. Sift the flour and celery salt into a food processor, add the butter and process until the mixture resembles fine breadcrumbs. Tip the mixture into a large bowl and add the walnuts and just enough cold water to bring the dough together.

❁ Turn out onto a floured surface and cut the dough in half. Roll out the first piece and cut out six 9-cm/3^1/$_2$-inch rounds. Take each round and roll out to 12 cm/4^1/$_2$ inches in diameter and fit into the muffin tin, pressing to fill the hole. Do the same with the remaining dough. Put a piece of baking paper in each hole and fill with baking beans, then leave to chill in the refrigerator for 30 minutes. Meanwhile, preheat the oven to 200°C/400°F/Gas Mark 6.

❁ Remove the muffin tin from the refrigerator and bake the tartlets blind in the preheated oven for 10 minutes, then carefully remove the paper and beans.

❁ Melt the butter in a frying pan, add the celery and leek and cook for 15 minutes, until soft. Add the 2 tablespoons of cream and crumble in the cheese, then mix well and season to taste with salt and pepper. Bring the remaining cream to a simmer in a separate pan, then pour onto the egg yolks, stirring all the time. Mix in the cheese mixture and spoon into the pastry cases. Bake for 10 minutes, then turn the tin around in the oven and bake for a further 5 minutes. Leave to cool in the tin for 5 minutes before serving.

Smoked Salmon, Dill & Horseradish Tartlets

Salmon has been smoked in Ireland for many centuries using traditional smoking techniques that capture and enhance both the flavour and texture of this fantastic fish. If you're short of time, you can use ready-made shortcrust pastry in this recipe.

Makes 6

Pastry
125 g/4$\frac{1}{2}$ oz plain flour, plus extra for dusting
pinch of salt
75 g/2$\frac{3}{4}$ oz cold butter, cut into pieces, plus extra for greasing

Filling
125 ml/4 fl oz crème fraîche
1 tsp creamed horseradish
$\frac{1}{2}$ tsp lemon juice
1 tsp capers, chopped
3 egg yolks
200 g/7 oz smoked salmon trimmings
bunch of fresh dill, chopped, plus extra sprigs to garnish
salt and pepper

❖ Grease six 9-cm/3$\frac{1}{2}$-inch loose-based fluted tartlet tins. Sift the flour and salt into a food processor, add the butter and process until the mixture resembles fine breadcrumbs. Tip the mixture into a large bowl and add just enough cold water to bring the dough together.

❖ Turn out onto a floured surface and divide into 6 equal-sized pieces. Roll each piece to fit the tartlet tins. Carefully fit each piece of pastry in its case and press well to fit the tin. Roll the rolling pin over the tin to neaten the edges and trim the excess pastry. Put a piece of baking paper in each tin, fill with baking beans and chill in the refrigerator for 30 minutes. Meanwhile, preheat the oven to 200°C/400°F/Gas Mark 6.

❖ Bake the tartlet cases blind in the preheated oven for 10 minutes, then carefully remove the paper and beans.

❖ Meanwhile, put the crème fraîche, horseradish, lemon juice and capers into a bowl with salt and pepper to taste and mix well. Add the egg yolks, smoked salmon and chopped dill and carefully mix again. Divide this mixture among the tartlet cases and return to the oven for 10 minutes. Leave to cool in the tins for 5 minutes before serving, garnished with dill sprigs.

Garlic & Herb Dublin Bay Prawns

Dublin Bay prawns are part of the lobster family and are also known as langoustines or scampi. Fresh Dublin Bay prawns are available outside Ireland, but if you can't find them you can use raw jumbo prawns instead. This dish is delicious served with a glass of chilled white wine.

Serves 2

12 raw Dublin Bay prawns in their shells
juice of 1/2 lemon
2 garlic cloves, crushed
3 tbsp chopped fresh parsley
1 tbsp chopped fresh dill
3 tbsp softened butter
salt and pepper
lemon wedges and crusty bread,
  to serve

❇ Rinse the prawns. Devein, using a sharp knife to slice along the back from the head end to the tail and removing the thin black intestine.

❇ Mix the lemon juice with the garlic, herbs and butter to form a paste. Season well with salt and pepper. Spread the paste over the prawns and leave to marinate for 30 minutes. Meanwhile, preheat the grill to medium.

❇ Cook the prawns under the preheated grill for 5–6 minutes. Alternatively, heat a frying pan and fry the prawns until cooked. Turn out onto warmed plates and pour over the pan juices. Serve immediately with lemon wedges and crusty bread.

DUNLUCE CASTLE, COUNTY ANTRIM

Potted Crab

'Potting' is a method from pre-refrigeration days for preserving all sorts of meat and fish. More recently, it has become a way of stretching extravagant ingredients a little further. The food is packed into small pots and covered with a layer of melted butter or other fat to exclude the air.

Serves 4–6

1 large cooked crab, prepared by your
   fishmonger if possible
whole nutmeg, for grating
2 pinches of cayenne pepper or mace
juice of 1 lemon
225 g/8 oz lightly salted butter
salt and pepper
buttered toast, to serve

- If the crab is not already prepared, pick out all the meat, taking great care to remove all the meat from the claws.

- Mix together the white and brown meat but do not mash too smoothly. Season well with salt and pepper and add a good grating of nutmeg and the cayenne pepper. Add the lemon juice to taste. Melt half the butter in a saucepan and carefully mix in the crabmeat. Turn the mixture out into 4–6 small soufflé dishes or ramekins.

- In a clean saucepan, heat the remaining butter until it melts, then continue heating for a few moments until it stops bubbling. Allow the sediment to settle and carefully pour the clarified butter over the crab mixture. This seal of clarified butter allows the potted crab to be kept for 1–2 days. Chill in the refrigerator for 1–2 hours.

- Serve with buttered toast.

Chapter 2
MAIN COURSES

Corned Beef & Cabbage

This dish is traditionally eaten in the United States to celebrate Saint Patrick's Day. In the past, the brining liquid may have included saltpetre, a bactericide that also produces the characteristic colour. Saltpetre is no longer available to the general public, but you may be able to buy brine mix from a good butcher.

Serves 6–8

4 litres/7 pints water
700 g/1 lb 9 oz coarse salt or brine mix
1.5 kg/3 lb 5 oz brisket, silverside or
   topside of beef
12 black peppercorns
4 cloves
3 bay leaves
1 large onion, sliced
6 carrots, cut into chunks
1 turnip, thickly sliced
6 large potatoes, cut into chunks
1 Savoy or green cabbage, cored and
   cut into wedges
2 tbsp chopped fresh parsley
mustard, to serve

✸ Pour the water into a large plastic or ceramic container and chill in the refrigerator for 1 hour. Stir in the salt until it has dissolved completely, then add the meat, making sure that it is completely submerged.

✸ Put the container in the refrigerator and leave for 7–10 days. Check daily that the meat is still submerged and skim off any foam that rises to the surface.

✸ Drain the meat, discarding the soaking liquid, then rinse. Put the meat into a large saucepan, add the peppercorns, cloves and bay leaves and pour in enough water to cover. Bring to the boil, skimming off any foam that rises to the surface. Reduce the heat, cover and simmer gently for 1³/₄ hours.

✸ Add the onion, carrots, turnip and potatoes to the pan, re-cover and simmer for 30 minutes. Add the cabbage and parsley, re-cover and simmer for a further 15–30 minutes, until the meat is tender.

✸ Remove the beef, cover with foil and leave to stand for 10 minutes to firm up. Strain the vegetables and put them into a warmed serving dish, discarding the peppercorns, cloves and bay leaves. Carve the meat into slices and serve immediately with the vegetables and mustard.

Beef in Stout with Herb Dumplings

Stout is a strong, dark beer that originated in the British Isles. The most famous Irish stout is Guinness, which is made from roasted, malted barley, hops, yeast and water. In this hearty stew, topped with light and fluffy suet dumplings, tender chunks of slow-cooked beef are enveloped in a rich gravy.

Serves 6

Stew
2 tbsp sunflower oil
2 large onions, thinly sliced
8 carrots, sliced
4 tbsp plain flour
1.25 kg/2 lb 12 oz stewing steak,
  cut into cubes
425 ml/15 fl oz stout
2 tsp muscovado sugar
2 bay leaves
1 tbsp chopped fresh thyme
salt and pepper

Herb Dumplings
115 g/4 oz self-raising flour
pinch of salt
55 g/2 oz shredded suet
2 tbsp chopped fresh parsley, plus extra
  to garnish
about 4 tbsp water

❦ Preheat the oven to 160°C/325°F/Gas Mark 3. Heat the oil in a flameproof casserole. Add the onions and carrots and cook over a low heat, stirring occasionally, for 5 minutes, or until the onions are softened. Meanwhile, place the flour in a polythene bag and season well with salt and pepper. Add the stewing steak to the bag, tie the top and shake well to coat. Do this in batches, if necessary. Reserve any remaining seasoned flour.

❦ Remove the onions and carrots from the casserole with a slotted spoon and reserve. Add the stewing steak to the casserole, in batches, and cook, stirring frequently, until browned all over. Return all the meat and the onions and carrots to the casserole and sprinkle in the reserved seasoned flour. Pour in the stout and add the sugar, bay leaves and thyme. Bring to the boil, cover and cook in the preheated oven for 1³/₄ hours.

❦ To make the herb dumplings, sift the flour and salt into a bowl Stir in the suet and parsley and add enough of the water to make a soft dough. Shape into small balls between the palms of your hands. Add to the casserole and return to the oven for 30 minutes. Remove and discard the bay leaves. Serve immediately, sprinkled with parsley.

Irish Stew

This robust stew was traditionally made using lamb or mutton (meat from a sheep over 1 year old), potatoes, onions and sometimes carrots. It is a white stew, meaning that the meat is not browned. If you have time, make it a day in advance because this will allow the delicious flavours to blend together.

Serves 4

4 tbsp plain flour
1.3 kg/3 lb middle neck of lamb, trimmed of visible fat
3 large onions, chopped
3 carrots, sliced
450 g/1 lb potatoes, quartered
1/2 tsp dried thyme
850 ml/1 1/2 pints hot beef stock
salt and pepper
2 tbsp chopped fresh parsley, to garnish

❁ Preheat the oven to 160°C/325°F/Gas Mark 3. Place the flour in a polythene bag and season well with salt and pepper. Add the lamb to the bag, tie the top and shake well to coat. Do this in batches, if necessary. Arrange the lamb in the base of a casserole.

❁ Layer the onions, carrots and potatoes on top of the lamb.

❁ Sprinkle in the thyme and pour in the stock, then cover and cook in the preheated oven for 2 1/2 hours. Garnish with the parsley and serve straight from the casserole.

HALFPENNY BRIDGE, DUBLIN

Pot-roast Pork

Pork has long been a popular meat in Ireland. In this tasty dish, tender pork loin is slowly braised in cider and stock. The resulting cooking liquid is then enriched with cream to create a delicious sauce.

Serves 4

1 tbsp sunflower oil
55 g/2 oz butter
1 kg/2 lb 4 oz boned and rolled pork loin joint
4 shallots, chopped
6 juniper berries
2 fresh thyme sprigs, plus extra to garnish
150 ml/5 fl oz dry cider
150 ml/5 fl oz chicken stock or water
8 celery sticks, chopped
2 tbsp plain flour
150 ml/5 fl oz double cream
salt and pepper
freshly cooked peas, to serve

- Heat the oil with half the butter in a heavy-based saucepan or flameproof casserole. Add the pork and cook over a medium heat, turning frequently, for 5–10 minutes, or until browned. Transfer to a plate.

- Add the shallots to the saucepan and cook, stirring frequently, for 5 minutes, or until softened. Add the juniper berries and thyme sprigs and return the pork to the saucepan with any juices that have collected on the plate. Pour in the cider and stock, season to taste with salt and pepper, then cover and simmer for 30 minutes. Turn the pork over and add the celery. Re-cover the pan and cook for a further 40 minutes.

- Meanwhile, make a beurre manié by mashing the remaining butter with the flour in a small bowl. Transfer the pork and celery to a platter with a slotted spoon and keep warm. Remove and discard the juniper berries and thyme. Whisk the beurre manié, a little at a time, into the simmering cooking liquid. Cook, stirring constantly, for 2 minutes, then stir in the cream and bring to the boil.

- Slice the pork and spoon a little of the sauce over it. Garnish with thyme sprigs and serve immediately with the celery, peas and the remaining sauce.

Potato, Leek & Chicken Pie

The humble pie is a mainstay of Irish cuisine, being as versatile as it is delicious. This modern take on the traditional chicken and leek pie uses filo pastry to give it a crispy topping. Unlike many pies, it is the perfect dish for a summer's day because it is light and not at all stodgy.

Serves 4

225 g/8 oz waxy potatoes, cubed
100 g/3½ oz butter
1 skinless chicken breast fillet, about
   175 g/6 oz, cubed
1 leek, sliced
150 g/5½ oz chestnut mushrooms,
   sliced
2½ tbsp plain flour
300 ml/10 fl oz milk
1 tbsp Dijon mustard
2 tbsp chopped fresh sage
225 g/8 oz filo pastry, thawed if frozen
salt and pepper

❧ Preheat the oven to 180°C/350°F/Gas Mark 4. Cook the potatoes in a saucepan of boiling water for 5 minutes. Drain and set aside.

❧ Melt half the butter in a frying pan and cook the chicken for 5 minutes, or until browned all over.

❧ Add the leek and mushrooms and cook for 3 minutes, stirring. Stir in the flour and cook for 1 minute, stirring constantly. Gradually stir in the milk and bring to the boil. Add the mustard, sage and potatoes, season to taste with salt and pepper and simmer for 10 minutes.

❧ Meanwhile, melt the remaining butter in a small saucepan. Line a deep pie dish with half of the sheets of filo pastry. Spoon the chicken mixture into the dish and cover with 1 sheet of pastry. Brush the pastry with a little of the melted butter and lay another sheet on top. Brush this sheet with melted butter.

❧ Cut the remaining filo pastry into strips and fold them onto the top of the pie to create a ruffled effect. Brush the strips with the remaining melted butter and cook in the preheated oven for 45 minutes, or until golden brown and crisp. Serve hot.

Fisherman's Pie

Fish pie is a popular everyday comfort food, and it can be a very fine dish when made with good-quality, fresh ingredients. The rich, creamy sauce and the addition of prawns and fresh herbs add to the luxury feel, making this a dish worthy of gracing any table.

Serves 6

900 g/2 lb white fish fillets, such as plaice, skinned
150 ml/5 fl oz dry white wine
1 tbsp chopped fresh parsley, tarragon or dill
175 g/6 oz small mushrooms, sliced
100 g/3$\frac{1}{2}$ oz butter, plus extra for greasing
175 g/6 oz cooked peeled prawns
40 g/1$\frac{1}{2}$ oz plain flour
125 ml/4 fl oz double cream
900 g/2 lb floury potatoes, cut into chunks
salt and pepper

❊ Preheat the oven to 180°C/350°F/Gas Mark 4. Grease a 1.7-litre/3-pint baking dish.

❊ Fold the fish fillets in half and place in the dish. Season well with salt and pepper, pour over the wine and scatter over the herbs.

❊ Cover with foil and bake in the preheated oven for 15 minutes, until the fish starts to flake. Strain off the liquid and reserve for the sauce. Increase the oven temperature to 220°C/425°F/Gas Mark 7.

❊ Sauté the mushrooms in a frying pan with 15 g/$\frac{1}{2}$ oz of the butter and spoon over the fish. Scatter over the prawns.

❊ Heat 55 g/2 oz of the remaining butter in a saucepan and stir in the flour. Cook for a few minutes without browning, then remove from the heat and add the reserved cooking liquid gradually, stirring well between each addition.

❊ Return to the heat and gently bring to the boil, stirring to ensure a smooth sauce. Add the cream and season to taste with salt and pepper. Pour over the fish in the dish and smooth over the surface.

❊ Cook the potatoes in a large saucepan of boiling salted water for 15–20 minutes. Drain well and mash with a potato masher until smooth. Season to taste with salt and pepper and add the remaining butter, stirring until melted.

❊ Pile or pipe the potato onto the fish and sauce and bake for 10–15 minutes, until golden brown.

Fish Cakes

Home-made fish cakes are a popular offering in seaside pubs, and their flavour is in a completely different league to that of the bland frozen fish cakes you may have eaten as a child. You can vary the fish according to what is available — a mixture of fresh and smoked fish would provide a sophisticated touch.

Serves 4

450 g/1 lb floury potatoes, cut into
  chunks
450 g/1 lb mixed fish fillets, such as cod
  and salmon, skinned
2 tbsp chopped fresh tarragon
grated rind of 1 lemon
2 tbsp double cream
1 tbsp plain flour
1 egg, beaten
115 g/4 oz breadcrumbs, made from
  day-old white or wholemeal bread
4 tbsp vegetable oil, for shallow-frying
salt and pepper
watercress and lemon wedges, to serve

- Cook the potatoes in a large saucepan of boiling salted water for 15–20 minutes. Drain well and mash with a potato masher until smooth.

- Put the fish in a frying pan and just cover with water. Place over a medium heat and bring to the boil, then reduce the heat, cover and simmer gently for 5 minutes, until cooked.

- Remove from the heat and drain the fish onto a plate. When cool enough to handle, flake the fish into large chunks, ensuring that there are no bones.

- Mix the potatoes with the fish, tarragon, lemon rind and cream. Season well with salt and pepper and shape into 4 large patties or 8 smaller ones.

- Dust the patties with flour and dip them into the beaten egg. Coat thoroughly in the breadcrumbs. Place on a baking tray and leave to chill in the refrigerator for at least 30 minutes.

- Heat the oil in the frying pan and fry the patties over a medium heat for 5 minutes on each side, turning them carefully using a palette knife or a fish slice.

- Serve with the watercress, accompanied by lemon wedges for squeezing over the fish cakes.

Winter Vegetable Cobbler

While a cobbler can be a fruit dessert similar to a crumble, any cobbler dish found on the menu in an Irish pub is more likely to be savoury rather than sweet. Cobblers are typically meat stews topped with thick rounds of scone dough, with each round forming a separate 'cobble'. This is a vegetarian version.

Serves 4

1 tbsp olive oil
1 garlic clove, crushed
8 small onions, halved
2 celery sticks, sliced
225 g/8 oz swede, chopped
2 carrots, sliced
1/2 small cauliflower, broken into florets
225 g/8 oz mushrooms, sliced
400 g/14 oz canned chopped tomatoes
55 g/2 oz red lentils
2 tbsp cornflour
3–4 tbsp water
300 ml/10 fl oz vegetable stock
2 tsp Tabasco sauce
2 tsp chopped fresh oregano, plus extra
  sprigs to garnish

Cobbler Topping
225 g/8 oz self-raising flour
pinch of salt
55 g/2 oz butter
115 g/4 oz mature Cheddar cheese,
  grated
2 tsp chopped fresh oregano
1 egg, lightly beaten
150 ml/5 fl oz milk

❖ Preheat oven to 180°C/350°F/Gas Mark 4.

❖ Heat the oil in a large flameproof casserole and cook the garlic and onions for 5 minutes. Add the celery, swede, carrots and cauliflower, and cook for 2–3 minutes. Add the mushrooms, tomatoes and lentils. Mix together the cornflour and water and stir into the casserole with the stock, Tabasco and chopped oregano.

❖ Cover the casserole, then transfer to the preheated oven and bake for 20 minutes.

❖ To make the cobbler topping, sift the flour and salt into a bowl. Rub in the butter, then stir in most of the cheese and the chopped oregano. Beat the egg with the milk and add enough of the mixture to the dry ingredients to make a soft dough. Knead lightly, roll out to a thickness of 1 cm/1/2 inch and cut into 5-cm/2-inch rounds.

❖ Remove the dish from the oven and increase the temperature to 200°C/400°F/Gas Mark 6. Arrange the scones around the edge of the dish, brush with the remaining egg and milk and sprinkle with the reserved cheese. Cook for a further 10–12 minutes, or until the topping is golden brown. Garnish with oregano sprigs and serve.

Chapter 3

VEGETABLES & SIDES

Colcannon

Colcannon is a traditional Irish dish often served at Halloween. In some families, the cook will hide lucky charms or coins in the mixture – these are said to bring the recipients good luck or fortune. This version uses cabbage and spring onions, but you can use kale and leeks instead if you prefer.

Serves 4

450 g/1 lb floury potatoes, cut into chunks
55 g/2 oz butter
150 ml/5 fl oz single cream
1/2 small green or white cabbage
6 spring onions, finely chopped
salt and pepper

- Cook the potatoes in a large saucepan of boiling salted water for 15–20 minutes. Drain well and mash with a potato masher until smooth. Season to taste with salt and pepper, add the butter and cream and stir well. The potato should be very soft.
- Cut the cabbage into quarters, remove the centre stalk and shred the leaves finely. Cook the cabbage in a large saucepan of boiling salted water for just 1–2 minutes, until it is soft. Drain thoroughly.
- Mix the potato and cabbage together and stir in the spring onions. Season well with salt and pepper.
- Serve in individual bowls.

THATCHED COTTAGES, COUNTY WATERFORD

Potato Cakes

Potato cakes used to be a way of using up leftover potatoes, but it is worth making some fresh mashed potatoes for this recipe because this will make the cakes particularly light and tasty. They are delicious served hot and smothered with butter.

Serves 4

550 g/1 lb 4 oz floury potatoes, cut into chunks
25 g/1 oz butter, plus extra to serve
1 egg (optional)
115 g/4 oz plain flour
oil, for greasing
salt and pepper

❧ Cook the potatoes in a large saucepan of boiling salted water for 15–20 minutes. Drain well and mash with a potato masher until smooth. Season to taste with salt and pepper and add the butter. Mix in the egg, if using.

❧ Turn the mixture out into a large mixing bowl and add enough of the flour to make a light dough. Work quickly as you do not want the potato to cool too much.

❧ Place the dough on a lightly floured surface and roll out carefully to a thickness of 5 mm/$\frac{1}{4}$ inch. Using a 6-cm/2$\frac{1}{2}$-inch pastry cutter, cut into rounds.

❧ Brush a flat griddle or heavy-based frying pan with oil and heat. Slip the potato cakes onto the griddle in batches and cook for 4–5 minutes on each side, until they are golden brown.

❧ Serve immediately with butter.

Glazed Turnips

Ireland's wet climate makes it the perfect place to grow turnips. This much underrated root vegetable is best picked while still small when the flavour is delicate and slightly sweet. The taste gets stronger as turnips age and the texture becomes coarser, sometimes woody.

Serves 4–6

900 g/2 lb young turnips, peeled and
  quartered
55 g/2 oz butter
1 tbsp soft light brown sugar
150 ml/5 fl oz vegetable stock
1 sprig of fresh rosemary
salt and pepper
chopped fresh parsley and grated
  orange rind, to garnish

❈ Put the turnips into a saucepan of boiling salted water, bring back to the boil and simmer for 10 minutes. Drain well.

❈ Melt the butter in the rinsed-out saucepan over a low heat, add the turnips and sugar and mix to coat well.

❈ Add the stock with the rosemary and bring to the boil. Reduce the heat and simmer for 15–20 minutes with the lid off the pan so that the juices reduce and the turnips are tender and well glazed.

❈ Remove the pan from the heat, discard the rosemary and season to taste with salt and pepper.

❈ Serve immediately, garnished with the chopped parsley and grated orange rind.

BOTANIC GARDENS, BELFAST

Sweet & Sour Red Cabbage

Cabbage is a vegetable that is particularly associated with Ireland, although it is only in the last century that so many different varieties have been available. In this tasty recipe, red cabbage is cooked with apples and flavoured with spices.

Serves 6–8

1 red cabbage, about 750 g/
   1 lb 10 oz
2 tbsp olive oil
2 onions, finely sliced
1 garlic clove, chopped
2 small cooking apples, peeled, cored
   and sliced
2 tbsp muscovado sugar
½ tsp ground cinnamon
1 tsp crushed juniper berries
whole nutmeg, for grating
2 tbsp red wine vinegar
grated rind and juice of 1 orange
2 tbsp redcurrant jelly
salt and pepper

❀ Cut the cabbage into quarters, remove the centre stalk and shred the leaves finely.

❀ Heat the oil in a large saucepan and add the cabbage, onions, garlic and apples. Stir in the sugar, cinnamon and juniper berries and grate a quarter of the nutmeg into the pan.

❀ Pour over the vinegar and orange juice and add the orange rind.

❀ Stir well and season to taste with salt and pepper. The saucepan will be quite full but the volume of the cabbage will reduce during cooking.

❀ Cook over a medium heat, stirring occasionally, until the cabbage is just tender but still has 'bite'. This will take 10–15 minutes, depending on how finely the cabbage is sliced.

❀ Stir in the redcurrant jelly, then taste and adjust the seasoning, adding salt and pepper if necessary. Serve immediately.

Honeyed Parsnips

In this recipe, oven roasting brings out the natural sweetness of the parsnips, which is then further enhanced by the addition of honey. These parsnips are the perfect accompaniment to any kind of roast meat.

Serves 4

8 parsnips, peeled and quartered
4 tbsp vegetable oil
1 tbsp honey

❈ Preheat the oven to 180°C/350°F/Gas Mark 4.

❈ Bring a large saucepan of water to the boil. Reduce the heat, add the parsnips and cook for 5 minutes. Drain thoroughly.

❈ Pour 2 tablespoons of the oil into a shallow ovenproof dish and add the parsnips. Mix the remaining oil with the honey and drizzle over the parsnips. Roast in the preheated oven for 45 minutes, until golden brown and tender. Remove from the oven and serve.

Irish Soda Bread

Soda bread has long been a staple in Ireland. It is a bread made without yeast, the raising agent being bicarbonate of soda mixed with buttermilk. A cross is cut into the top of the bread to help it rise and, according to Irish folklore, to either ward off evil or to let the fairies out.

Makes 1 loaf

vegetable oil, for oiling
450 g/1 lb plain flour, plus extra for
 dusting
1 tsp salt
1 tsp bicarbonate of soda
400 ml/14 fl oz buttermilk

❧ Preheat the oven to 220°C/425°F/Gas Mark 7. Oil a baking tray.

❧ Sift the flour, salt and bicarbonate of soda into a mixing bowl. Make a well in the centre of the dry ingredients and pour in most of the buttermilk. Mix well together using your hands. The dough should be very soft but not too wet. If necessary, add the remaining buttermilk.

❧ Turn the dough out onto a lightly floured surface and knead it lightly. Shape into a 20-cm/8-inch round.

❧ Place the loaf on the prepared baking tray and cut a cross into the top with a sharp knife. Bake in the preheated oven for 25–30 minutes, until golden brown and it sounds hollow when tapped on the bottom. Transfer to a wire rack and leave to cool slightly. Serve warm.

TRIM CASTLE, COUNTY MEATH

Oat & Potato Bread

This recipe uses freshly cooked potatoes, but it is also a wonderful way to use up leftover mashed potatoes. It makes a dense, moist loaf that is the perfect accompaniment to any meal, although it is particularly delicious served with a traditional Irish fried breakfast.

Makes 1 loaf

vegetable oil, for oiling
225 g/8 oz floury potatoes
  (peeled weight)
500 g/1 lb 2 oz strong white flour,
  plus extra for dusting
1½ tsp salt
40 g/1½ oz butter, diced
1½ tsp easy-blend dried yeast
1½ tbsp soft dark brown sugar
3 tbsp rolled oats
2 tbsp skimmed milk powder
210 ml/7½ fl oz lukewarm water

Topping
1 tbsp water
1 tbsp rolled oats

❊ Oil a 900-g/2-lb loaf tin. Put the potatoes in a large saucepan, add water to cover and bring to the boil. Cook for 20–25 minutes, until tender. Drain, then mash until smooth. Leave to cool.

❊ Sift the flour and salt into a warmed bowl. Rub in the butter with your fingertips. Stir in the yeast, sugar, oats and milk powder. Mix in the mashed potato, then add the water and mix to a soft dough.

❊ Turn out the dough onto a lightly floured work surface and knead for 5–10 minutes, or until smooth and elastic. Put the dough in an oiled bowl, cover with clingfilm and leave to rise in a warm place for 1 hour, or until doubled in size.

❊ Turn out the dough again and knead lightly. Shape into a loaf and transfer to the prepared tin. Cover and leave to rise in a warm place for 30 minutes. Meanwhile, preheat the oven to 220°C/425°F/Gas Mark 7.

❊ Brush the surface of the loaf with the water and carefully sprinkle over the oats. Bake in the preheated oven for 25–30 minutes, or until it sounds hollow when tapped on the bottom. Transfer to a wire rack and leave to cool slightly. Serve warm.

Barm Brack

Barm Brack is a yeast bread with added sultanas and raisins — it is sweeter than standard bread but not as rich as cake. It is traditionally eaten around Halloween, when charms are baked into the dough as part of an ancient fortune-telling ritual.

Makes 1 loaf

650 g/1 lb 7 oz strong white flour,
  plus extra for dusting
1 tsp mixed spice
1 tsp salt
2 tsp easy-blend dried yeast
1 tbsp golden caster sugar
300 ml/10 fl oz lukewarm milk
150 ml/5 fl oz lukewarm water
vegetable oil, for oiling
4 tbsp softened butter, plus extra
  to serve
325 g/11½ oz mixed dried fruit (golden
  raisins, currants and raisins)
milk, for glazing

❅ Sift the flour, mixed spice and salt into a warmed bowl. Stir in the yeast and caster sugar. Make a well in the centre and pour in the milk and water. Mix well to make a sticky dough. Turn the dough out onto a lightly floured work surface and knead until no longer sticky. Put the dough in an oiled bowl, cover with clingfilm and leave to rise in a warm place for 1 hour, until doubled in size.

❅ Turn the dough out onto a floured work surface and knead lightly for 1 minute. Add the butter and dried fruit to the dough and work them in until completely incorporated. Return the dough to the bowl, replace the clingfilm and leave to rise for 30 minutes.

❅ Oil a 23-cm/9-inch round cake tin. Pat the dough to a neat round and fit in the tin. Cover and leave in a warm place until it has risen to the top of the tin. Meanwhile, preheat the oven to 200°C/400°F/Gas Mark 6.

❅ Brush the top of the loaf lightly with milk and bake in the preheated oven for 15 minutes. Cover the loaf with foil, reduce the oven temperature to 180°C/350°F/Gas Mark 4 and bake for a further 45 minutes, until golden brown and it sounds hollow when tapped on the bottom. Transfer to a wire rack and leave to cool.

Savoury Oat Crackers

These crunchy oat crackers, with added walnuts and sesame seeds, are quick and easy to make. They would be the ideal accompaniment for a cheese board – make sure to include a range of Irish cheeses and some pickles or chutney.

Makes 12–14

100 g/3½ oz unsalted butter, plus extra
   for greasing
90 g/3¼ oz rolled oats
25 g/1 oz plain wholemeal flour
½ tsp coarse sea salt
1 tsp dried thyme
40 g/1½ oz walnuts, finely chopped
1 egg, beaten
40 g/1½ oz sesame seeds

❈ Preheat the oven to 180°C/350°F/Gas Mark 4. Lightly grease two baking trays.

❈ Rub the butter into the oats and flour using your fingertips. Stir in the salt, thyme and walnuts, then add the egg and mix to a soft dough. Spread out the sesame seeds on a large shallow plate or tray. Break off walnut-sized pieces of dough and roll into balls, then roll in the sesame seeds to coat lightly and evenly.

❈ Place the balls of dough on the prepared baking trays, spacing well apart, and roll the rolling pin over them to flatten. Bake in the preheated oven for 12–15 minutes, or until firm and pale golden. Transfer to a wire rack and leave to cool.

GIANT'S CAUSEWAY, COUNTY ANTRIM

Chapter 4

DESSERTS & DRINKS

Bread & Butter Pudding

Warm and comforting, bread and butter pudding is the perfect dessert for a cold winter's day. It was traditionally made with dry leftover bread, but this luxury version uses fresh bread — you could also try using fruit bread.

Serves 4–6

85 g/3 oz butter, softened
6 slices thick white bread
55 g/2 oz mixed dried fruit
  (sultanas, currants and raisins)
25 g/1 oz candied peel
3 large eggs
300 ml/10 fl oz milk
150 ml/5 fl oz double cream
55 g/2 oz caster sugar
whole nutmeg, for grating
1 tbsp demerara sugar

❧ Preheat the oven to 180°C/350°F/Gas Mark 4.

❧ Use a little of the butter to grease a 20 x 25-cm/8 x 10-inch baking dish and the remainder to butter the slices of bread. Cut the bread diagonally into quarters and arrange half overlapping in the prepared baking dish.

❧ Scatter half the dried fruit and peel over the bread, cover with the remaining bread slices and add the remaining dried fruit and peel.

❧ In a mixing jug, whisk the eggs well and mix in the milk, cream and caster sugar. Pour this over the pudding and leave to stand for 15 minutes to allow the bread to soak up some of the egg mixture.

❧ Tuck the dried fruit and peel under the bread slices so that they don't burn. Grate a little of the nutmeg over the top of the pudding, according to taste, and sprinkle over the demerara sugar.

❧ Place the dish on a baking tray and bake at the top of the oven for 30–40 minutes, until just set and golden brown. Remove from the oven and serve warm.

Apple Cake

Apples have been grown in Ireland for many centuries — legend has it that St Patrick himself planted an apple tree in an ancient settlement outside Armagh city. Today, Armagh County is known as 'Orchard County' and celebrates its apples with festivals and apple blossom tours. This cake is a tasty way of using apples and can be served warm for dessert.

Serves 8

450 g/1 lb cooking apples
175 g/6 oz self-raising flour
1 tsp ground cinnamon
pinch of salt
115 g/4 oz butter, plus extra for
  greasing
115 g/4 oz caster sugar
2 eggs
1–2 tbsp milk
icing sugar, for dusting

Streusel Topping

115 g/4 oz self-raising flour
85 g/3 oz butter
85 g/3 oz caster sugar

❧ Preheat the oven to 180°C/350°F/Gas Mark 4. Grease a 23-cm/ 9-inch round springform cake tin.

❧ To make the streusel topping, sift the flour into a bowl and rub in the butter until the mixture resembles breadcrumbs. Stir in the caster sugar and reserve.

❧ Peel, core and thinly slice the apples. To make the cake, sift the flour into a bowl with the cinnamon and salt. Place the butter and caster sugar in a separate bowl and beat together until light and fluffy. Gradually beat in the eggs, adding a little of the flour mixture with the last addition of egg. Gently fold in half the remaining flour mixture, then fold in the rest with the milk.

❧ Spoon the mixture into the prepared tin and smooth the top. Cover with the sliced apples and sprinkle the streusel topping evenly over the top. Bake in the preheated oven for 1 hour, or until browned and firm to the touch. Leave to cool in the tin before removing the sides. Dust the cake with icing sugar before serving.

Rhubarb Crumble

This comforting and homely dessert is incredibly simple to make —
you can even make the crumble topping a day or so in advance and
store it in the refrigerator until you are ready to use it. For an extra-
crunchy topping, use demerara sugar in place of the light brown sugar.

Serves 6

900 g/2 lb rhubarb
115 g/4 oz caster sugar
grated rind and juice of 1 orange
cream, yogurt or custard, to serve

Crumble Topping
225 g/8 oz plain white or
   wholemeal flour
115 g/4 oz unsalted butter
115 g/4 oz soft light brown sugar
1 tsp ground ginger

❧ Preheat the oven to 190°C/375°F/Gas Mark 5.

❧ Cut the rhubarb into 2.5-cm/1-inch lengths and place in a 1.7-litre/
3-pint ovenproof dish with the caster sugar and the orange rind
and juice.

❧ To make the crumble topping, sift the flour into a bowl. Rub in
the butter with your fingertips until the mixture resembles fine
breadcrumbs. Stir in the brown sugar and the ginger. Spread evenly
over the fruit and press down lightly using a fork.

❧ Place the dish on a baking tray and bake in the preheated oven for
25–30 minutes, until the crumble is golden brown. Serve warm with
cream, yogurt or custard.

DOO LOUGH, COUNTY MAYO

Blackberry Soup with Buttermilk Custards

Although dried carrageen (Irish moss) would traditionally have been used as a thickening agent for custards and milk puddings, this recipe uses the more readily available gelatine. The sweet and inky blackberry soup and wobbly buttermilk custards are a sublime combination.

Serves 4

Buttermilk Custards
4 sheets leaf gelatine
275 ml/9$\frac{1}{2}$ fl oz buttermilk
275 ml/9$\frac{1}{2}$ fl oz double cream
50 ml/2 fl oz milk
100 g/3$\frac{1}{2}$ oz caster sugar

Blackberry Soup
450 g/1 lb blackberries
300 ml/10 fl oz fruity red wine
100 ml/3$\frac{1}{2}$ fl oz water
75 g/2$\frac{3}{4}$ oz caster sugar, or to taste
2 star anise
4–5 tbsp blackberry liqueur (optional)

❧ To make the custards, put the gelatine in a small bowl, cover with cold water and leave to soak for 5 minutes. Meanwhile, heat the buttermilk, cream and milk together in a saucepan to just below boiling point. Add the sugar and stir until it has completely dissolved. Remove the gelatine from the soaking liquid and squeeze out any excess water. Add to the hot buttermilk mixture and stir until completely dissolved. Pour through a fine sieve and fill four dariole moulds or individual pudding moulds. Transfer to the refrigerator and chill for several hours, or overnight, until set.

❧ To make the blackberry soup, put the blackberries, wine and water in a large saucepan with the sugar and star anise. Simmer very gently for 8–10 minutes, until the sugar has dissolved and the mixture has a lovely anise scent. Remove from the heat and leave to cool. Once the mixture has cooled, remove and discard the star anise, transfer the mixture to a food processor and blend until smooth. Pour through a fine sieve and stir in the liqueur, if using. Cover and chill in the refrigerator until ready to serve.

❧ To serve, divide the blackberry soup between four soup plates (rather than deep bowls) and place a buttermilk custard in the centre of each.

Irish Cream Cheesecake

This is an unbaked cheesecake and, although it contains no gelatine, its high chocolate content ensures that it sets perfectly. It is a luxurious dessert that is made even more special by the addition of Irish Cream, a popular liqueur made from Irish whisky, coffee and cream.

Serves 8

vegetable oil, for oiling
175 g/6 oz chocolate chip cookies
55 g/2 oz unsalted butter
crème fraîche and fresh strawberries,
    to serve

Filling

225 g/8 oz plain chocolate, broken
    into pieces
225 g/8 oz milk chocolate, broken
    into pieces
55 g/2 oz golden caster sugar
350 g/12 oz cream cheese
425 ml/15 fl oz double cream,
    lightly whipped
3 tbsp Irish Cream liqueur

❀ Line the base of a 20-cm/8-inch round springform cake tin with baking paper and brush the sides with oil. Place the cookies in a polythene bag and crush with a rolling pin. Put the butter in a saucepan and heat gently until melted. Stir in the crushed cookies. Press into the base of the prepared cake tin and chill in the refrigerator for 1 hour.

❀ Put the plain and milk chocolate into a heatproof bowl set over a saucepan of gently simmering water until melted. Leave to cool. Put the sugar and cream cheese in a bowl and beat together until smooth, then fold in the cream. Fold the melted chocolate into the cream cheese mixture, then stir in the liqueur.

❀ Spoon into the cake tin and smooth the surface. Leave to chill in the refrigerator for 2 hours, or until quite firm. Transfer to a serving plate and cut into slices. Serve with crème fraîche and strawberries.

Irish Coffee

Irish coffee is a cocktail made with strong, hot coffee, Irish whiskey and sugar, topped with thick cream. It is the perfect way to round off a meal or to ward off the night's chill. You'll need a steady hand to get the cream to float on top, but practice makes perfect!

Serves 1

2 measures Irish whiskey
1 tsp sugar, or more to taste
freshly made strong black coffee
2 measures double cream

❧ Put the whiskey into a warmed heatproof glass with sugar to taste.

❧ Pour in the coffee and stir until the sugar has completely dissolved. Pour the cream very slowly over the back of a spoon that is just touching the top of the coffee and the edge of the glass. Keep pouring until all the cream is added and has settled on the top.

❧ Do not stir – drink the coffee through the cream.

TORC WATERFALL, COUNTY KERRY

Black Velvet

This beer cocktail is made using equal measures of stout and sparkling white wine (traditionally Guinness and champagne). The different densities of the liquids mean that they should, in theory at least, remain in separate layers, as in a pousse-café. For a Poor Man's Black Velvet, use cider instead of the wine, pouring it into the glass first and floating the stout on top.

Serves 1

stout, chilled
sparkling white wine, chilled

Half-fill a tumbler with stout, then very slowly pour in an equal quantity of wine over the back of a spoon that is just touching the top of the stout and the edge of the glass. This should prevent the drinks from mixing together too much and help to keep them in separate layers. Serve immediately.

BUNRATTY FOLK PARK, COUNTY CLARE

Index